En l'air

a collection of poems created in the air
by Pamela Herron

2013 Unsolicited Press Trade Paperback Edition

Published in the United States by Unsolicited Press.

ISBN: 0615894526

ISBN-13: 9780615894522

Dedication

To my husband Albert Wong for love and sustenance;
to my first and best reader, my son, Thomas Michael Herron Stover;
and in memory of my mother, Janie Elizabeth Reynolds Herron,
who always believed.

Table of Contents

Poems

En l'air

Flying in the air
gazing below at raw earth
see the tracks of man

Sore suburban sprawl
ravaged mountains and rivers
insignificant

Of poor stewardship
of responsibility
unseen importance

Visible damage
bulldozed, drained, forever lost
inflicted by us

In my youth, I danced
soaring above silken wood
lost in the music

En l'air, to dance free
unfettered by earthly bonds
touch, leap without care

Flying, in the air
out a plastic sealed window
the earth condemns us

En l'air, free once more
to care, to serve, to wonder
belong with the earth

Poem from above

Cotton wisps
flickering
past my window
a dream world
castle in the sky.

Little boxes,
blocks,
dominoes
curvy paths in
ordered squares

Illusion
of an unplanned
development
Monopoly squares,
a board game

Rumpled blankets
still warm
barren hills
now verdant green
humped over the plain

Rugged height
smoothed to
distant tracing
soft horizon, a glow
beyond the curve of the earth

Emerald lakes,
hills, valleys, reduced to
a child's world
etched in a puddle
after a rain

Looking down
past the wing

a shadow flying
a child's tracing
on paper

Rounds of green
metal arms
crop circles
an offering
a libation

Our message
to unknowns who
watch from the galaxies.
We spend water to
appease our gods.

Flight to Philadelphia

We fly because we must.
T-shirt, flip-flops bound for SoCal
Not me.
Padded coat, gloves, woolen undies
The snow blows where I'm going.
Clouds stretch as far as the desert sands.

A short sleep and sandy browns give way
Snow-crème, sugar-coated jagged fragments
Connected by threads of grey.
Horizon fades to a haze of palest azure.

Snow-covered puzzle pieces
On a sky-blue tablecloth.
Barges scattered like crumbs.
Orange and blue Southwest flying south below us.
Ashy bits of land held fast in estuary ice.
Salty fresh water still and March cold.
Tiny rivers and creeks frozen in time as they flow to the sea.

Wings dip and the sun winks.
Late afternoon rays slice across the sugar dusted plain
Furry five o' clock shadow illumined by a warming light.
Glare sparkles on the plastic oval scratched by a thousand winter storms
Evergreens warm and dusky below keep the snow warm until spring.

Oval tracks, curvy lines, a stick tracing
One V of flying geese, landing gear down, cut through the light
A sweep of faded blue with a spray of white
Chesapeake Bay. New Jersey Causeway.
Sliced sheet cake, knife edge straight
Nubs of silos, greenhouse rows
Ward off the winter

Scraggly branches
Sparse as an old man's comb-over
Wait for spring
Metal roof flashes, deep inverted V echoes air travelers

In the spring
Birds and planes fly
Against coming spring
Criss-cross crops, corn rows, a farm ochre and drab
Sleep until spring

Mud-caked flats
Crags of a wizened face
Give way to eight lanes
Oil refineries by the river
Piers for no fishermen
Checkerboard Purina
The cereal of a nation
Guards the sweep of grey
Philly airport.

Desert Blues

Powder blue sky
cloudless, pale
but for a sweep of
vermilion lined with
sable velvet,
brushed from below by
pinon and juniper.

Moments later,
like wild geese a-wing,
scarlet has faded
to dusky grey.
Wisps
fade above the
rumpled mountains.

Powder blue
pallor deepens
to Wedgewood.
A smudge of silk
remains as lights
twinkle on
one by one.

Wedgewood
fades fast to
smoke.
Midnight
savours enough
blue to tint the
morning before dawn.

The Acacia

Acacia tree
Saffron flowers amid thorns
A breath of iris

Desert flowering
Animals shelter with thorns
Sweet scent through the night

Rain sage *morjado*
Flower on dusty grey-green
Waiting for the storm

Red rock, rolling hills
Dusted with a fur of green
After the night rain

Yellow flowers fall
Shriven by the evening storm
Seed pods born anew

Desert Dawn

Storm cloud awakens
Lightning disturbs my slumber
Tomorrow blossoms

Sierra Nevada Spinal Fusion Elegy

(The following collection of five poems developed from journals while my only sister began a long recovery from spinal surgery (24 November – 1 December 2008). Many early mornings found me gazing out the window across frozen fields with the craggy mountains surrounding Lake Tahoe rising through the mist.)

Sustained – Sostenuto – 24 November

Fruit trees raise their dormant grasp
silhouettes against the sky

Cloudless cerulean bowl
shelters tired white-headed peaks

Dried leaves, remnants of summer
rattle on branches and twigs

Chismosas con soldado – Sinestra - 26 November

At the edge
of a back yard,
a swarm of quail
scurry and scramble
for snacks in the grass.

No dignity, no pride
the bustle of Thornton Burgess'
Mrs. Bob White but
more like overweight
shoppers shoving
at a Thanksgiving sale.

One stops to pull
at the grass,
and twelve more
press and push
to get some too.

Red pinnacled
heads bobbing
against the faded
yellow sagebrush.
one alien visitor,
no crest,
long pointed beak.

He came
scattering the flock
all running
so quickly,
their plump bodies
skim over
valleys and humps.

They do not fly
all gone now.
grey skies hang heavy.
snow on Tahoe

a whisper of
winter to come.
The field
is still,
empty,
then one
by one,
they return.

Wary,
watching
one
by one
they land
but
the stranger
                    still
                              waits.

Sleeping Clay – Sempre -- November 29

Silver wraiths hover
tonsure below weary heads
Points iced with night snow

Iced evening snow lifts
jagged points above mounds soft
green rumpled blankets.

Grey head nods above
sleeping face, reflect, preying
death and the dying.

Siege - Staccato - November 30

Ranks of pines
erect soldiers
point to the heavens
and glimpse
signs passing below
Cave Rock
Zephyr Cove
Round Hill
Elk Point
a warning of deer
bear crossing.

snowy peaks
watch over
blue hills
Tahoe still
glassy
surface reflects
mountains mirrored
deep in the water
deeper than the sky.

The lean
hungry
road
threads through
the muffled pines
we climb
higher
and yet
higher

Morning Melt – Smorzando - December 1

One dewdrop glistens
reflecting and refracting
morning dawns anew

Hoary tips weeping
kissed by sparkling sun, the grass
a diamond bed

Eastern light spangled
a vapor trail, wisp of smoke
disappears above

Sagebrush emerges
from the frost, Venus rises,
pale, blond wraithe appears

A hawk glides above
riding over unseen waves
of airborne currents

With a sweep of wings
he banks to the mountaintop.
People unaware

Farmer at the barn
never looks up, never sees
his breath gusts white clouds

Sandstone worn away
to rusty red in the dawn
Sunlight sweeps glazed grass

Frosted sagebrush, stiff
in the glassy morning air
waits, a touch of warmth

Faint vapor trails criss
cross the celestial span,
fatten, fan and fade

Four blackbirds appear
swoop and dive, scold descending
then rest on the wire.

Night Flight

Dusky night shadow
Sparrow wing brushes the night
Weary, flying home.

Hooded yellow eyes
Head tilts a silent click east
Quiet and watchful.

A breath of movement
Wings spread in nightshade drop
Deadly silent strike

Bright eyes closed, asleep
Sun rises on empty nest
Scattered feathers drift.

Swans

Swans
mate for life,
they say.
What biological imperative
demands
Monogamy?

Humans,
on the other hand,
desire
Monogamy,
but cannot
get it right.

The swan,
neck curved,
watches
over her
grey, fuzzy
cygnets.

While the male
wings outspread,
defends his
battleship group
from perceived
danger.

A child kneels alone to watch.
The small armada sails home.
Bread cast upon
still water
unseen,
unwanted.

Mocking Bird

I never understood my father,
except perhaps
when I was a child.
Then he was
protective
all-powerful.

Snow drifts
against
cold grey stone.
A bit of ribbon,
faded
plastic rose.

Mockingbird
swoops, dives,
wings splayed
tail spread.
A fat robin
has ventured too close.

His mate
hovers near
their nest
watching every move
prepared to battle
if needed.

Summer
will come.
Nestlings will fly.
I hear the mockingbird
morning song until
time to build again.

Outside my childhood window
the mockingbird sang
morning awake
I walked the fields
with my father
once again.

Bright
warm nest
with bits of ribbon
and faded
flowers.
Mockingbird sings.

Keeping Time

My mother watched
kept time for the family.
Wearily rising
from her chair,
rocker creaking a refrain,
she picked up Big Ben,
began winding,
and told us
good night
go to bed.

Sometimes she fooled
herself and set the clock
ten minutes fast as
though she could
cheat time.
She never could.
There were other Big Bens.
Little ones, then bigger ones
with bigger numbers
glowing softly through the night.

She wound the clock for
the factory whistle,
the school bus,
for early rehearsals,
and me.

She never
wound the clock
for herself.

She kept time
faithfully.
Waiting, watching
the morning dawn
on a tipsy daughter,
the one who slipped away,
the man who stayed out
too late for no reason.

And we all came home.
And she would wind
the clock for another day.
Our house never needed an electric clock.
One with a snooze alarm
or a radio
to wake us with music.
I remember
she never slept.
No need for a clock
ticking forward to a milky dawn.
None of us ever had our own
clock to wind and wake
us in the morning.

But every evening,
she rose from
the hand-woven reeds of
the wooden rocking chair,
walked to the tall table
with the bills
and the Bible,
and wind the clock

Today the clack
of a winding clock
brings me back.
But of course,
no one winds
clocks today.

Numbers glow
red and evil
throughout
the night and
I wonder
how could she
sleep with that damn
Big Ben ticking away
the hours at the head of her bed.

Marking time
for all of us.
My dual alarms
wake us all,
separately, and
no one
winds the clock.
Nine volts
watch the time
even in a storm.

My pink
cell phone
has an alarm,
numbers that
glow in the dark, and
music.
To remind me
of meetings,
names and numbers
of my friends
and family.
Never needs winding.
It doesn't tick.

When she died,
I kept her watch,
the Timex,
the one I bought her,
with the big numbers,
after the little ones
danced and drifted
before her eyes.
I wore the watch,
big black numbers
marking time
for me,
until it stopped.

Remembrance

I have touched the sun
smoothed it warm upon your hair
not yet forgotten.

Worn face, tired lines
silver hairs catch the sunlight
your eyes sing within.

Tattered photographs
falling from a worn Bible
speak of days gone by.

Sleep. The long tarewell.
Death holds little mystery
for the ones who wait.

Love Letters

A box of letters
dried flowers
capture a love lost
long ago.

Ink
on paper
a promise
to always be there

Love always,
the words
remain
written in the past

A stain for
ever
alters
the future

Lament

Notes and reminders fade
swept away
buried ideas
dust on a forgotten shelf

Lost
in a drift
of letters
bills,

First Class
Open Immediately!
Act Now!
or lose.

Words
enter
your mind
a gift

An omen
an offering
one time only
special offer

Not redeemed
laid aside
meant
to be written

Do the words
settle upon
the thoughts
of someone else?

Or are they
lost
forever
yours.

Time - Haiku for Life

Birth
Early morning light
Lonely darkness, hands, eyes clenched
Hungry, thirsty, wet.

Youth
Spring fever. No sleep.
He loves me. He loves me not.
No one understands.

Working
Promotion today
Early bird catches the worm
Brush off resume.

Middle age
Morning dawn awake
Burning eyes, wandering mind
No caffeine past noon.

Golden years
Listen to the birds
Listen for someone to call
Too much time. Wasted.

Remembrance
To relive it all
Time for them, for you, for me
Silence for all time.

Lostwords

Words thought, wrought, and lost
Tangled in cyberspace. Gone
Should have emailed, saved

Search complete.
no results to display.
Misnamed, unsaved, lost.

Thin cold envelope.
We regret to inform you
Undesirable

Dreams rejected

Rainwords

When they fall into your hands like raindrops
or like snowflakes, perfect and crystalline
only to melt with the warmth of your fingertips.

Words fall like rain, gentle, soft, warm
Words fall like rain, a torrential downpour
Smashing and washing away
Houses, roads and bridges.

What gets left behind?
Words become memory
lodged in someone else's mind

Legacy does not
always let you choose
Nor does it always
Choose you.

. . . . *and I think of China.*

Great Wall
Forbidden City
Terra Cotta Soldiers
Temple of Heaven
Middle Kingdom
Tourists gape,
with cameras,
from air-conditioned buses,
thinking they've seen China.
Trapped in a dining hall
lazy susan with fries.

And they think they've seen China

Yangtze lazes
brown and deep
cutting centuries
through the mountains.
Ordered terraces on the hillside,
gathered lace of orange trees,
melons and greens.
Dinner still warm from the sun.
Basket hat masks the face
unchanging
for centuries.

And I think of China

Security police, so very young,
crisp uniform, eyes forward,
Unblinking.
See the foreigner
looking at you?
To see if you are looking at me?
Red Guard kerchief
treasured at home
Did you ever giggle
or play?
Will your children?

And I think of China

Hutongs
hidden alleys
sizzle an evening meal.
An old man in cotton shorts
fans himself, sees me
and stops.
He nods
and fans again.
Women with baskets of fruit
walk home with no hand to fan.
Children laugh behind grey walls

And I think of China

China has always been,
in ways unknown
To occidentals.
Robert Hooke in 1666
decreed the sun of the western sky
occido - Latin to go down or set.
The sun has set on the Silk Road,
Artists, philosophers, inventors, writers,
5000 years before Mr. Hooke
oriented China in the East..
Winds change

And I think of China

Historic
Beijing,

Ancient
Xian,

Modern
Shanghai,

Bustling
Hong Kong,

Stone forests
Great deserts
Rivers run through

And I think of China

China cares
what we think,
But they don't have to.
Do we care
what they think?
We will have to.
China closed doors for centuries,
because they could.
Can we open doors to the future,
because we should?
It won't always be ours to choose.

And I think of China

Golden years,
golden glow
on the bay,
Mist creeping over *Lantau,*
Incense and temple bells
America?
China?
America.
China.
I long for home,
a peaceful ending

and I think of China

Bless the Beasts

Consider
the lilies of the field,
as we toil and
spin through life.
Flowers don't quarrel,
except for Lewis Carroll.

Wolves
mate for life,
golden eagles, swans, cranes.
We snarl and snap
without consideration
of a greater good.

Children of wolves
the pack supports
the single parent.
Single people-parent
walk alone only by the grace of
human destruction.

Condors and coyotes,
prairie voles
and vultures.
Even termites stay
together during
their quest for their nests.

Bless the beasts
and if
the beasts
are blessed,
why not
our children?

Bombs or Bake Sales, again?

Bumper sticker today,
on bombs and bake sales,
tattered and faded,
fluttering in the wind.

Like a missile launched,
who can stop
what was begun years ago
on a fractured,
fragile world
grown smaller today.

Last meal,
last request
a dying planet.
Shall it be quick,
in a blossoming mushroom cloud?
Or shall we spend
lifetimes
in exquisite misery,
torturing
here today and
gone tomorrow?

You can choose.
Every action, a reaction
Think about it.

Think about
every word you say.
Think about
everything you do.
Think about
everyone you meet,
or don't meet.

They were children once too.
A bake sale?
Let them eat cake.
Off with their heads.

You choose
every day
every moment.

What are you thinking
right
now.

www.ingramcontent.com/pod-product-compliance
Lightning Source LLC
LaVergne TN
LVHW050947080826
845145LV00004B/1449

* 9 7 8 0 6 1 5 8 9 4 5 2 2 *